The Marriage Course

MANUAL

Alpha

Alpha Resources
Alpha North America

Published in North America by Alpha North America, 74 Trinity Place, New York, NY 10006

© 2000 Alpha International, Holy Trinity Brompton, Brompton Road, London, SW7 1JA, UK

The Marriage Course Manual

First printed by Alpha North America in 2002

Printed in the United States of America

Cover design by Button Design
Illustrations by Charlie Mackesy

ISBN 10: 1-931808-50-3
ISBN 13: 978-1-931808-50-7

12 13 14 15 16 Printing/Year 11 10 09 08 07

Contents

SESSION 1

Building Strong Foundations

WHAT IS MARRIAGE?

INTRODUCTION

- a man and a woman joined together

- a relationship of growing interdependence

THE FOUR SEASONS OF MARRIAGE

(not every marriage will go through each stage—but the principles apply to all marriages)

1. Spring

- married without children

- on average about two years

- full of anticipation and excitement

- the greatest need is to accept each other

2. Summer

- family with children under the age of 12

- length 12 years

"For this reason a man will leave his father and mother and be united to his wife, and they will become one flesh."
Genesis 2:24

Jesus said, "So they are no longer two but one."
Matthew 19:6

- busy and tiring
- the greatest need is to give time to the marriage relationship

3. Autumn

- family with teenage children at home
- approximate length 10-15 years
- changeable and sometimes stormy
- the greatest need is to support and encourage each other

4. Winter

- frequently lasts more than 20 years—the longest of the seasons
- probably less active with an opportunity for more time together
- the greatest needs are shared interests and good communication

WHY DO SOME MARRIAGES BREAK DOWN?

- a process of growing apart
- a lack of communication (poem: "The Wall")
- consumerism—the failure to work at a relationship

Notes

_____

_____

_____

_____

_____

_____

_____

_____

_____

_____

_____

_____

_____

_____

_____

_____

_____

_____

_____

_____

_____

_____

Marriage:
the closest possible human relationship of growing interdependence

Notes

_____

_____

_____

_____

_____

"Love and faithfulness meet together."
Psalm 85:10

THE AIM OF THE MARRIAGE COURSE

- to help couples grow closer
  - through commitment
  - through time together
  - through a greater understanding of each other
  - through developing good habits

THE MARRIAGE WHEEL

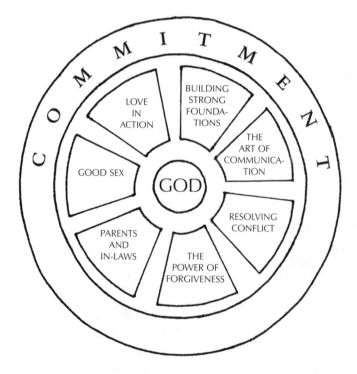

EXERCISE 1 – Taking stock of your marriage

Please read through the list of statements and, using the scale below, write in the box the number which you feel corresponds to your viewpoint. (where 0 = never true, 1 = rarely true etc.). Please do the exercise on your own. When you have finished, Total each of the four columns marked A, B, C, D and then **turn over the page**.

0. never true **1**. rarely true **2**. occasionally true **3**. usually true **4**. always true

I feel that ...   A   B   C   D

1. My partner regularly gives me his/her undivided attention___☐

2. My partner understands and supports my beliefs and values___☐

3. My partner shows me affection through demonstrative non-sexual touching___☐

4. We are able to apologize and forgive each other when one of us has hurt the other___☐

5. My partner listens to my point of view even when we disagree ___☐

6. I am able to talk to my partner about my sexual hopes and desires ___☐

7. I am able to talk to my partner about my dreams and aspirations for the future ___☐

8. My partner is good at encouraging me in what I do___☐

9. We make a priority of going out together at least once every 2 weeks___☐

10. We often reflect on the good things we enjoy as a couple___☐

11. We are able to talk about strong emotions such as excitement, hope, grief, and anxiety___☐

12. My partner is sensitive toward my sexual needs___☐

13. My partner encourages me in my spiritual growth___☐

14. My partner is good at meeting my emotional needs___☐

15. We agree on our sexual practices___☐

16. We discuss new ideas with each other ___☐

17. We support each other in the goals we have for our family life___☐

18. We have a number of joint interests that we pursue together ___☐

19. I am happy about the frequency of our lovemaking ___☐

20. My partner is good at listening to my feelings without interrupting or criticizing me___☐

TOTALS: A ☐ B ☐ C ☐ D ☐

(Turn page to continue)

Results of "Taking stock of your marriage"

1. Transfer your total scores for A, B, C, D from the previous page

	My score	**Partner's score**
A = **Building our friendship**	☐	
B = **Building our communication**	☐	
C = **Building our physical relationship**	☐	
D = **Building our future together**	☐	

2. Now look at each other's scores and discuss them, especially any differences.
(The idea is to be understood by and to understand each other better.)

3. Husbands, tell your wife something in each area that you would like to see changed in yourself. Wives then do the same.

For example:

Friendship: *"I see that I haven't recognized the need for us to spend time together on our own. What could I do to change that?"*

Communication: *"I don't seem to be very good at listening. I obviously need to show you that I am interested in what you say."*

Physical relationship: *"I would like to be more sensitive toward your sexual desires. What could I do?"*

The future: *"We haven't had a conversation for a long time about our plans for the future. When would be a good time for that?"*

Making time for each other

To build a close lifelong marriage relationship we need to give time to each other on a regular basis.

Unless we deliberately set aside time for each other each week, we'll discover that the demands of work, parenting, finances, and many other everyday disruptions and distractions, or simply taking each other for granted, will stop us being close.

Plan to spend, at the very least, one–two hours alone together each week to rekindle romance, to have fun, to talk together about your feelings (e.g., your hopes, fears, worries, excitements). We call this *marriage time.*

The aim of marriage time is:

- to keep the romance alive
- to deepen our understanding and appreciation of each other
- to ensure we communicate regularly on a meaningful level

Marriage time builds intimacy.

Notes

_____

_____

_____

_____

_____

_____

_____

_____

_____

_____

_____

_____

_____

_____

_____

_____

_____

_____

_____

_____

_____

_____

_____

Notes

How to make marriage time happen:

1. Plan time together

It doesn't happen automatically. Find the best time for you.

Write it in your planners, e.g., Monday evening—"Marriage Time" or Wednesday lunchtime—"Marriage Time" or Saturday breakfast—"Marriage Time." If the time needs to be different each week, plan a month ahead, and, if you are very busy, several months in advance.

2. Prioritize your time together

"Prioritizing marriage time is constantly the most difficult thing that we struggle to do, but the most important in terms of how it impacts our relationship."
Couple on *The Marriage Course*.

3. Protect your time together

Protect this time from interruptions and distractions such as the telephone, visitors, the television, and over-long working hours.

NURTURING ONE ANOTHER

1. Love is more than feelings

- a definition of love—meeting the needs or desires of another, sometimes at a cost to ourselves

- the greatest need of our husband or wife is to feel understood and loved

2. God created us with a need for close human relationships

- marriage designed to counter aloneness

- nurture one another by meeting emotional needs

- nurturing builds trust

3. Proactive versus reactive

- reactive means focusing on each other's behavior

- proactive means focusing on each other's desires

- when we feel loved we feel like loving

"The Lord God said, 'It is not good for the man to be alone. I will make a helper suitable for him.'"
Genesis 2: 18

Notes

"Husbands, live with your wives in an understanding way."
1 Peter 3:7

4. Study each other

- the same but different

- discovering what matters to our husband or wife

- otherwise we tend to give what we like to receive

- desires change over time

- make requests not demands

EXERCISE 2 – "Knowing me, knowing you"

Please read through the list on the next page:

1. In column A, check the three that matter most to you (i.e., that you would most like your husband or wife to give to you).

2. In column B, check the three that you believe matter most to your husband or wife (i.e., that you think they would most like to receive from you).

Note: There is some overlap between the different desires—put those three which most clearly express your preferences.

3. When you have both finished, exchange your responses and see how well you understand your husband or wife.

- *How close were you to selecting the three that matter most to your husband or wife?*

- *How many of the same desires did you and your partner put for yourselves? 0? 1? 2? 3?*

- *Consider which, if any, of the list of desires you tend to **give least** to your husband or wife. Are these any of the three that matter most to your partner?*

	A myself (choose 3)	B my partner (choose 3)
Affirmation – being appreciated for who you are by your partner	☐	☐
Approval – being commended for those things you have done well	☐	☐
Companionship – doing things together and sharing experiences	☐	☐
Conversation – talking together about issues of interest and importance	☐	☐
Encouragement – being inspired to keep going through your partner's words	☐	☐
Openness – being confident of your partner's honesty about every aspect of their lives, including their feelings and ideas	☐	☐
Physical affection – the communication of care and closeness through physical touch	☐	☐
Practical help – experiencing your partner's help in big or small tasks	☐	☐
Presents – receiving tangible expressions of love and thoughtfulness	☐	☐
Respect – having your ideas and opinions considered and valued by your partner	☐	☐
Security – facing the future confident of your partner's commitment to love you and stay with you	☐	☐
Sexual intimacy – having regular opportunities to express and receive love through your sexual relationship	☐	☐
Support – knowing your partner is working with you to fulfill your goals	☐	☐
Time together – knowing your partner has set aside time to be with you on a regular basis	☐	☐
Understanding – knowing your partner is aware of what matters to you	☐	☐
Undivided attention – focusing on each other to the exclusion of any distractions	☐	☐

Marriage Time Homework

Set aside two hours of Marriage Time together sometime before the next session for the following two exercises.

EXERCISE 1 – Planning to succeed

Each of you write down your answers to the following questions. When you have both finished, show each other what you have written and then discuss your answers.

A. Time together

(1) How much time do you set aside to spend alone together to build your marriage. . .

on a daily basis?

_____

on a weekly basis?

_____

on an annual basis?

_____

(2) How much time could you be spending together regularly, and when. . .

on a daily basis?

e.g., 20 minutes to talk together when we get home in the evening or 10 minutes in the morning to plan the day

on a weekly basis?

e.g., every Friday night to go out together or Monday evening to spend at home talking over a meal

_____

on an annual basis?

e.g., go away for a long weekend as a couple or have an annual mini-honeymoon

_____

B. Shared interests

(1) What interests do you have in common? (Think back to what you did when you first went out together.)

e.g., visiting art galleries, playing a sport, exploring new places, going to the movies

_____

_____

_____

_____

_____

(Turn page to continue)

(2) Which of these interests do you pursue together as a couple now?

How regularly?

How much time do you set aside for them?

e.g., playing tennis—once every two weeks—two hours (complete your answers on page 16)

_____

_____

_____

_____

(3) Are there other mutual interests you would benefit from pursuing together now?

_____

_____

_____

_____

C. Separate interests

(1) What interests do you encourage your partner to pursue that you do not share?

_____

_____

_____

_____

(2) What interests do you pursue that your partner does not share?

_____

_____

_____

(3) Are there other separate interests that you or your partner would like to pursue?

You: _____

_____

Your partner: _____

_____

D. Annual Vacations

(1) Which have been your best vacations together and why?

_____

_____

_____

(2) Suggest an idea for a vacation/time away together in the future.

_____

_____

_____

_____

(Turn page to continue)

EXERCISE 2 – Showing love

1. Write down what you remember to be your husband's or wife's top three desires from the exercise "Knowing me, knowing you" (page 13).

1._____ 2._____ 3._____

2. Now write down your own three main desires and give examples of how your husband or wife could meet them for you.

For example:

My desires	**How my partner could meet them**
Conversation	*Initiate conversation when we are having a meal together by asking me questions about my day.*
Approval	*Tell me when I have done something well at home or at work. Show that you notice when I have made an effort.*
Time together	*Take the initiative in suggesting we go out together. Sit down with me for 30 minutes each evening to talk about the day.*
Physical affection	*Hug and kiss me when we see each other after time apart. Hold me in bed before we go to sleep.*
Presents	*Give me a present when I least expect it.*

My desires   **How my partner could meet them**

1. _____

_____

_____

_____

2. _____

_____

_____

_____

3. _____

_____

_____

_____

- Show each other what you have written.
- In the coming weeks, try to concentrate on meeting your husband's or wife's desires rather than criticizing him or her for not meeting yours.

SESSION 2

The Art of Communication

Reminder

The aim of *The Marriage Course* is to establish patterns of relating that will keep marriages alive for a lifetime

Building strong foundations

- make marriage time a weekly priority in your planners

- meet your partner's desires (see "Knowing me, knowing you," page 13)

THE ART OF COMMUNICATION

INTRODUCTION

- intimacy requires effective communication

- *The Marriage Course* is all about communication both during and between the sessions

EFFECTIVE COMMUNICATION

- communication involves the message, the sender, and the receiver

- building intimacy in marriage involves hearing each other's experiences, thoughts, feelings, and desires

THE IMPORTANCE OF TALKING

- we need to tell each other thoughts and feelings

- some have been taught to hide feelings

- it takes courage and practice to re-learn to talk at this level

Notes

_____

_____

_____

_____

_____

_____

_____

_____

_____

_____

Barriers to talking

Notes

_____

_____

_____

_____

_____

_____

"My dear brothers and sisters, take note of this: Everyone should be quick to listen, slow to speak and slow to become angry."
James 1: 19

"Those who answer before listening —that is their folly and their shame."
Proverbs 18:13

_____

THE IMPORTANCE OF LISTENING

- most of us take listening for granted yet it is possible to close our ears

- we can be selective in our listening

- listening provides support

- listening requires effort

- the Bible places great stress on listening

- our own experience tells us that listening is important

EXERCISE 1 – The power of listening

Discuss the following questions as a couple:

- How does it feel when you are listened to?

- How does it feel when you are not listened to?

- To whom would you go to if you needed a listening ear?

- What makes that person a good listener?

HINDRANCES TO LISTENING

1. Filters

- all of us listen through filters but we are unaware of them most of the time

- when someone is speaking, our own expectations, prejudices, past experiences, values, beliefs, feelings, etc. all affect what we hear

- some of the time we are listening more to ourselves than to the other person

- effective communication requires us to control the conversation in our mind

(see diagram below)

Listening through filters

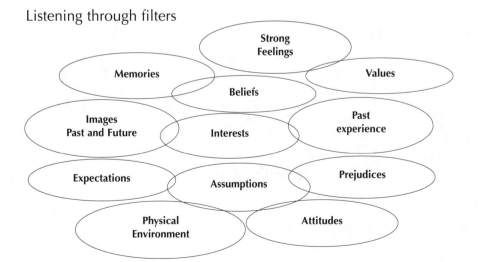

Notes

_____

_____

_____

_____

_____

_____

_____

_____

_____

2. Bad habits

- jumping in and reassuring
- giving advice
- intellectualizing/spiritualizing
- interrupting
- going off on a tangent
- such responses hinder the speaker from saying everything they need to say
- we need to wait until we have listened before coming in with our contribution

(see diagram below)

Deflective listening is defective listening

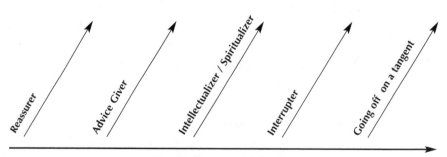

Speaker's concern/issue

EXERCISE 2 – A significant memory

Effective communication involves allowing our husband or wife to talk about their feelings.

- Take turns spending one minute telling your husband or wife about a happy memory of something that happened to you before you met.

- The listener should then summarize what he/she has heard, taking particular care to describe their partner's feelings. This will show that he/she has been listening and empathizing with what his/her partner felt.

PRINCIPLES FOR EFFECTIVE LISTENING

Learning to listen is for some people as difficult as learning a foreign language, but we must learn in order to grow closer to our husband or wife.

1. Pay attention and do not interrupt

Allow your partner to finish what he is saying. Research indicates that the average individual listens for only 17 seconds before interrupting. Maintain eye contact and do not do something else at the same time.

2. Put yourself in your partner's shoes

Put your own views to one side and really appreciate what it is like for your partner to be feeling the way that she does. This takes patience and compassion on the part of the listener. Do not ask a lot of questions. Try to tolerate silences.

Notes

_____

_____

_____

_____

_____

_____

_____

_____

_____

_____

"If I were to summarize in one sentence the single most important principle I have learned in the field of interpersonal relations, it would be this: Seek first to understand, then to be understood."
Steven Covey

Notes

_____

_____

_____

_____

_____

_____

_____

_____

_____

_____

_____

_____

_____

_____

_____

"The first service that one owes to others in fellowship consists in listening to them. Just as love of God begins with listening to His Word, so the beginning of love for the brethren is learning to listen to them."

Dietrich Bonhoeffer

3. Acknowledge their feelings

When you have listened to what your partner wants to say, reflect back what you heard without deflection or interpretation. It is important to try to summarize accurately the main facts but to reflect back the feelings in full. This helps your partner to know if you have understood. "Reflecting back" may feel awkward, but it works!

4. Find out what is most important

Then ask your husband or wife: *"What is the most important part of what you have been saying?"* Wait quietly while your partner thinks about what he wants to say. When he has spoken, reflect back again what you have heard.

5. Help her determine what she might do

Now ask: *"Is there anything you would like me/us to do about what you have said?"* Again give your partner time to think quietly. When he has finished, reflect back what your partner has said, enabling him to hear his own decision. The listener then asks, *"Is there anything more that you would like to say?"* If there is anything more, this should also be reflected back to the speaker.

EXERCISE 3 – Effective listening

Each of you pick an issue currently upsetting or bothering you that you have not previously discussed. At this point, choose an issue where there has not already been disagreement and conflict. It could be an area of concern related to work, vacations, children, your home, etc.

- The speaker should hold a handkerchief (or something similar). This is to remind you whose issue is being discussed.

- The speaker tells the listener about the issue and how he or she feels about it. The listener listens and then reflects back.

- Then the listener asks, *"What is the most important aspect of what you are saying?"* The speaker responds. The listener listens and then reflects back again.

- The listener then asks, *"Is there anything you would like to do* (or, if appropriate: *like me/us to do) about what you have just said?"* Again the listener listens and then reflects back.

- Finally, the listener asks, *"Is there anything more that you would like to say?"*

Then switch roles so each of you has a chance to speak and to listen. This exercise is good practice for all of us both in sharing our emotions and in listening to each other.

Marriage Time Homework

A. Each of you complete the exercise below, "How good is your communication?" Compare what you have written.

B. Then take an area in your marriage where you are not communicating with your partner and follow the steps for Exercise 3, "Effective listening" (page 27). Please ensure that both of you are ready to do this and are willing to follow the steps.

Follow the guidelines as listener and speaker as you work through each other's issue. Some of you may experience a strong emotional reaction to what your partner is saying. Try to put your own reaction to one side and keep listening and reflecting back what your partner is feeling.

EXERCISE – How good is your communication?

1. Areas in our relationship where, I think, we communicate well—i.e., we are both able to express our views and we understand each other well:

_____

_____

2. Areas where we do communicate, but not well enough—i.e., in my view, there is room for improvement:

_____

_____

_____

3. Areas where we are not communicating at all – whether through neglect, embarrassment, or fear:

_____

_____

_____

Suggested topics for consideration:

- Handling children

- Money matters

- Goals and directions in life

- Sex – frequency or quality

- Contraception/how many children

- Jobs around the home

- Death and bereavement

- Job or career/time at the office

- Church involvement

- Expressing affection and emotions

- Relaxation and rest

- Relatives and in-laws

SESSION 3

Resolving Conflict

Reminder

The aim of *The Marriage Course* is to establish patterns of relating that will keep marriages alive for a lifetime.

Building strong foundations

- make marriage time a weekly priority in your diaries

- meet your partner's desires (see "Knowing me, knowing you" page 13)

The art of communication

- talk about your feelings with your partner this week

- listen to your partner's feelings without interrupting, criticizing, or offering advice

RESOLVING CONFLICT

Notes

INTRODUCTION

- some conflict is inevitable

- we have different opinions

- we are naturally selfish

- we fail to handle anger properly

    – some are like rhinos—they attack when provoked

    – some are like hedgehogs —they withdraw when threatened

- unresolved conflict leads to "trench warfare"

FOUR PRINCIPLES FOR HANDLING CONFLICT

1. Expressing our appreciation of each other

- make it a daily discipline

- be thankful for what your partner does

- be appreciative for who your partner is

Turn to page 36 and fill in Exercise 1 – "Showing appreciation"

Notes

_____

_____

_____

_____

_____

_____

_____

_____

_____

_____

_____

_____

_____

_____

_____

_____

_____

"Accept one another then, just as Christ accepted you...."
Romans 15:7

"Why do you look at the speck of sawdust in the other person's eye and pay no attention to the plank in your own eye?"
Matthew 7:3

2. Recognizing our differences

- recognize differences of temperament, personality, background, and expectations

- don't try to change each other

- seek to complement each other

- look for each other's strengths

- support each other's weaknesses

Turn to page 37 and complete Exercise 2 - "Recognize your differences"

3. Negotiating areas of conflict

- negotiate rather than attack, surrender, or bargain

- six steps to peace

    (1) find the best time (the 10 o'clock rule)

    (2) identify the issue

    (3) discuss the issue rather than attacking each other

    – avoid labeling (e.g., "you never..." "you always...")

    – use "I" statements (e.g., "I feel undervalued when...")

    – listen to your partner (allow them to hold the handkerchief as described in Session 2)

– each express your views in turn

(4) work out the possible solutions (make a list if necessary)

(5) decide on the best solution for your relationship and see if it works

(6) be prepared to re-evaluate

Turn to pages 38-41 and complete Exercise 3 – "Changing our behavior"

4. Learning to pray together

1. Putting God at the center

When we expect our partner to meet all our needs, we inevitably fail each other and get hurt.
(See Diagram 1)

Diagram 1

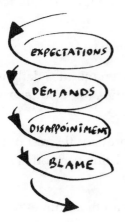

Notes

We were created to be in a relationship with God – only He can meet all our needs.
(See Diagram 2)

God

Husband → Wife

Diagram 2

2. Seeking God's way

Praying together as a couple will strengthen and sustain a marriage relationship over a lifetime and build intimacy.

Many marriages today involve a battle of the wills as husband and wife argue to get their own way. Christian marriage involves a couple seeking God's will together.

3. Getting started

- five to ten minutes daily is better than one hour every month

- don't pray for the rest of the world; bring each other's needs to God

- start with thankfulness

"Live as children of light... and find out what pleases the Lord."
Ephesians 5:8 and 10

"Therefore do not be foolish, but understand what the Lord's will is."
Ephesians 5:17

- listen and respond to each other's requests

- accept the same requests day after day

- ensure prayers are vertical not horizontal and manipulative

- don't give up—even with small children

- draw on God's promises from the Bible—try *30 Days* or *Daily Light*

- the closer each of us is individually in our relationship with God, the closer we are to each other as husband and wife

"A cord of three strands is not quickly broken."
Ecclesiastes 4:12 This describes a husband and wife with God at the center of the relationship. (To explore this further, consider doing an Alpha course together—see the final page for more information.)

Notes

_____

_____

_____

_____

_____

_____

_____

_____

_____

_____

_____

_____

_____

_____

_____

_____

_____

"Confess your faults to one another and pray for one another...."
James 5:16

"God is our refuge and strength, an ever-present help in trouble."

Psalm 46:1

EXERCISE 1 – Showing appreciation

Write down six expressions of appreciation about your husband or wife.
(Be specific: it may be thanking them for what they do, or it may be
expressing your appreciation for who they are—try to make it a
mixture—looking particularly for things you may have come to take for
granted.)

e.g.,   *I love the way you get along so well with other people.*

   I love the way you're so affectionate toward me.

   Thank you for working so hard to provide for our family.

   Thank you for making our home such a welcoming place to be.

   I appreciate it a lot that you fill the car up with gas.

1. _____

2. _____

3. _____

4. _____

5. _____

6. _____

EXERCISE 2 – Recognize your differences

1. Mark against each issue where on the line your partner's and your own preferences each lie. *e.g., (N = Nicky; S = Sila)*

Money   Spend   _____S_____N_____   Save

Punctuality   Have time in hand _____S_____N_____   Cut it close

2. Show each other what you have put. Then find one issue where your differences can be a source of strength for your relationship.

Issue:

Clothes	Casual	_____	Formal
Disagreements	Fight it out	_____	Keep the peace
Holidays	Seek adventure	_____	Seek rest
Money	Spend	_____	Save
People	Spend time with others	_____	Spend time alone
Planning	Make plans and stick to them	_____	Be spontaneous and go with the flow
Punctuality	Have time in hand	_____	Cut it close
Relaxation	Go out	_____	Be at home
Sleeping	Go to bed late	_____	Get up early
Sport	Enthusiast	_____	Uninterested
Telephone	Talk at length	_____	Make arrangements only
Tidiness	Keep everything tidy and under control	_____	Be relaxed and live in a mess
T.V.	Keep it on	_____	Throw it out

Other differences: _____

EXERCISE 3 – Changing our behavior

While we cannot change each other, we need to be prepared to change ourselves. This will include habits of our own which cause our partner unhappiness as well as angry reactions to our partner's habits.

Please spend a few minutes completing the following questions on your own.

1. Would you describe yourself as a "rhino" or a "hedgehog"?

(When upset or provoked, the rhino launches an attack while the hedgehog withdraws.)

_____

How would you describe your partner?

_____

2. What are the most important reasons for (a) frustration, resentment, hurt, or anger in you toward your partner? (b) frustration, resentment, hurt, or anger in your partner toward you?

(a) _____

(b) _____

3. (a) When you get angry with your partner, what do you usually do?

(b) When your partner gets angry with you, what does he/she usually do?

(a) _____

(b) _____

4. At times of disagreement, what words or phrases are you aware that you use, if any, that hurt your partner?

_____

_____

What words or phrases does your partner use, if any, that hurt you?

_____

_____

(This question is especially important if either or both of you recognize that you react like the rhino.)

5. (a) When you feel anger toward your partner, are there other ways in which you hurt him/her? *(e.g., walk away, shut them out, withhold sex)*
(b) When your partner feels anger toward you, are there other ways in which he/she hurts you?

(a) _____

(b) _____

(Turn page to continue)

6. At times of disagreement, are you and your partner able to express your views and feelings?

_____

If not, how could you help your partner to do so?

_____

(This question is especially important if either or both of you recognize that you react like the hedgehog.)

7. In disagreements do you feel that you and your partner try to see each other's viewpoint?

_____

If not, what could you do to listen to each other more effectively?

_____

8. What are the worst times of the day/week to talk about disagreements?

_____

What are the best times?

_____

9. When you disagree, do you focus on the issue or attack each other?

_____

What could help you focus on the issue?

_____

10. Are you able to practice the verse, *"Do not let the sun go down while you are still angry"* (**Ephesians 4:26**)? Before going to sleep each night, do you forgive each other for hurts arising from conflict even when the issue remains unresolved?

_____

Now look at and discuss each other's answers.

Marriage Time Homework

EXERCISE – Focusing on the issue

The purpose of this exercise is to discuss areas of conflict and to discover the best solutions together. Make sure you are not demanding but rather requesting changes in each other.

1. Each of you write down one issue that causes conflict in your marriage which arises from a habit or pattern of behavior **in you** that needs to be changed.

_____

_____

_____

2. What needs to happen for you to change this pattern of behavior?

_____

_____

_____

3. What could your partner do to help you to change?

_____

_____

_____

(Turn page to continue)

Now using the "six steps to peace" under "Negotiating areas of conflict" on pages 32 and 33 as a guideline, negotiate the areas of conflict that you each identified.

4. Our agreed mutually acceptable solution is

_____

_____

_____

5. Write down one issue that causes conflict in your marriage which arises from a habit or pattern of behavior in **your partner** that could be changed. Be specific and positive as you raise areas of importance to you.

For example: I would love it if you could be more affectionate when we meet after work. I wish we could stop criticizing each other in front of others/the children. I would appreciate it a lot if we could be more punctual.

_____

_____

_____

6. What could **your partner** do to change this pattern of behavior?

_____

_____

_____

7. What could you do to help your partner to change?
(Note: personal criticism, shouting, nagging, bullying, etc. are unhelpful)

_____

_____

_____

Again, using the "six steps to peace" under "Negotiating areas of conflict" on pages 32 and 33, negotiate the areas of conflict you each identified for point 5 above.

8. Our agreed mutually acceptable solution is

_____

_____

_____

9. Would you like to spend a few minutes praying together each day? If so, when and how could this best be achieved?

_____

_____

_____

SESSION 4

The Power of Forgiveness

Reminder

The aim of *The Marriage Course* is to establish patterns of relating that will keep marriages alive for a lifetime.

Building strong foundations

- make marriage time a weekly priority in your planners

- meet each other's desires (see "Knowing me, knowing you," page 13)

The art of communication

- talk about your feelings with your partner this week

- listen to your partner's feelings without interrupting, criticizing, or offering advice

Resolving conflict

- express your appreciation for your partner every day

- when you disagree, discuss the issue rather than attack each other

- plan to spend a few minutes each day praying with and for each other

THE POWER OF FORGIVENESS

HOW CAN INTIMACY BE LOST?

- intimacy is built on trust and openness

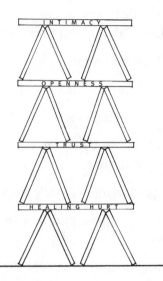

- hurt undermines trust and openness

- hurt is inevitable within every marriage

- some hurt will be unintentional

- reactions to hurt

  - anger (rhinos and hedgehogs)

  - retaliation and/or fear

  - resentment and/or guilt

Notes

WHAT HAPPENS IF HURT AND ANGER ARE BURIED?

- physical symptoms

  - disturbed sleep

  - appetite affected

  - medical conditions, e.g., ulcers, high blood pressure, pain

- affects behavior

  - inability to relax

  - low sexual desire

  - obsessive behavior, e.g., perfectionism

  - quick temper/intolerance

  - escape through drugs or alcohol

  - escape into work/children/ religious activities/ etc.

- emotional symptoms

  - loss of positive emotions, e.g., romance, love, joy

  - low self-esteem/depression

  - shut down

  - fear of confrontation

"In your anger do not sin. Do not let the sun go down while you are still angry, and do not give the devil a foothold."
Ephesians 4:26-27

How can intimacy be restored?

1. Identify the hurt

- recognize the ways in which you have caused your partner pain and hurt your marriage (See Matthew 5:23-24)

- be prepared to tell your partner where you have been hurt (See Matthew 18:15)

2. Apologize

- take responsibility

- resist the urge to rationalize what you did or to blame your partner

- confess to God

  – enables us to see the effect of our actions

- apologize to each other

  – love means often having to say we are sorry

  – opens the way for reconciliation and healing

Turn to pages 51-53 and complete the exercise—"Identifying unresolved hurt"

Notes

_____

_____

_____

_____

_____

_____

"Get rid of all bitterness, rage and anger...
Be kind and compassionate to one another, forgiving each other, just as in Christ God forgave you."
Ephesians 4:31-32

"Therefore, if you are offering your gift at the altar and there remember that your brother or sister has something against you, leave your gift there in front of the altar. First go and be reconciled to them; then come and offer your gift."
Matthew 5:23-24

"If your brother or sister sins against you, go and show them their fault, just between the two of you. If they listen to you, you have won them over."
Matthew 18:15

"If we confess our sins he is faithful and just to forgive us and to cleanse us from all unrighteousness."
1 John 1:9

Notes

_____

_____

_____

_____

_____

_____

_____

_____

_____

_____

_____

_____

_____

_____

_____

_____

_____

_____

_____

_____

_____

*"Father, forgive them for they know
not what they do."*
Luke 23:34

3. Forgive

- forgiveness is one of the greatest forces for healing in a marriage

- degrees of difficulty in forgiving

  – Jesus on the cross of those who crucified Him

  – range of forgiveness in marriage

  – small issues, e.g., forgetting to do something or making you late

  – big issues, e.g., unfaithfulness

- forgiveness first and foremost a choice not a feeling

- question is not

  – do we feel like forgiving?

- question is

  – will we forgive?

  – will we let go of our self-pity/ demand for justice/ desire to retaliate?

- new feelings follow forgiveness

- forgiveness **IS NOT**

  – demanding a person changes before we forgive them

  – forgetting the hurt happened

  – pretending it doesn't matter

- thinking time alone will heal the hurt

- forgiveness **IS**

  - facing the wrong done to us

  - recognizing the emotions inside

  - choosing not to hold it against our husband or wife

  - releasing him/her into God's hands

- forgiveness deals with anger and resentment—although we might still feel hurt until healing is complete

- forgiveness is a process—we often need to keep forgiving—sometimes on a daily basis

- my forgiveness may benefit my partner but ultimately I'm the one who benefits by being free from the bondage of bitterness

- we must let go of our anger and desire to retaliate even if our partner has not yet apologized to us—otherwise buried anger turns to hate

- "the flow of forgiveness"—we are to forgive out of gratitude for the forgiveness we have received

Notes

_____

_____

_____

_____

_____

_____

_____

_____

_____

_____

_____

_____

_____

"Peter came to Jesus and asked, 'Lord, how many times shall I forgive my brother or sister whey they sin against me? Up to seven times?' Jesus answered, 'I tell you, not seven times but seventy times seven.'"
Matthew 18:21-22

"Bear with each other and forgive whatever grievances you may have against one another. Forgive as the Lord forgave you."
Colossians 3:13

Notes

"Love keeps no record of wrongs."
1 Corinthians 13:5

"Confess your faults to one another and pray for one another that you may be healed."
James 5:16

"Forgetting what lies behind and pressing forward to what lies ahead."
Philippians 3:13

4. Start again together

- thank God for showing you your mistakes and for His forgiveness

- having gone through the process of identifying, apologizing and forgiving, cross out your lists of hurt as a sign that you have resolved them between you

- comfort each other—we make ourselves very vulnerable through this process and it is hard to listen to the ways in which we have hurt each other

- pray for one another—pray aloud or silently asking God to heal your partner of the hurt you have caused him or her

This process is like a drain that carries away the hurt. Confession to God and those we hurt, together with forgiving those who have hurt us, must become a daily habit if intimacy is to be maintained. Otherwise the drain begins to block up with unresolved hurt and anger.

EXERCISE – Identifying unresolved hurt

This exercise concentrates particularly on identifying the areas of hurt and seeking to understand each other's feelings better. The homework focuses on apology and forgiveness.

1. Try to identify your partner's hurt

Please think about any ways in which you have hurt your partner and affected your marriage that have not been resolved between you. Think back to when you were going out, engagement, and early marriage as well as recent times. (None of us is perfect.)

- *What have I failed to do that I should be doing?*
- *What have I done (or am I doing) that I should not do?*
- *Where have I failed to meet my husband's/wife's needs?*
- *What have I said that has been hurtful?*
- *What have I left unsaid that could have shown love and encouragement?*

Don't make excuses or blame your partner. The following examples show the difference:

Making excuses/blaming our partner:
I know I criticized you in front of the children yesterday, but I wouldn't have done so if you hadn't made us twenty minutes late.

Proper apology:
I hurt you by criticizing you in front of the children yesterday; it was unkind of me. I am sorry.

(Turn page to continue)

Making excuses/blaming our partner:
I know I was grumpy and rude toward you last night, but you don't understand what intense pressure I've been under at work for the last two weeks.

Proper apology:
It was selfish and insensitive of me to be rude and grumpy toward you last night. I am sorry to have hurt you.

Write a list of the things that come to mind. Be specific.

(For example: I have stopped being affectionate and rejected your initiatives to make love; I have fallen asleep in front of the television instead of talking with you; I have been out more consistently with work colleagues or friends than we have together as a couple; I said some very unkind things during that big argument we had two weeks ago about money.)

_____

_____

_____

_____

_____

2. Identify your own hurt

Identify the ways in which you have been hurt by your partner. The cause of the hurt could be recent or a long time ago. Your partner might or might not have been aware of hurting you and it could have been one incident or repeated many times. Make sure you are specific and that you describe how you felt. Use "I" sentences.

(For example: I felt unsupported and unappreciated when you didn't notice the hard work I put into decorating the house for Christmas; I was hurt when you didn't say anything special about my promotion; I haven't gotten over the fact that you lied to me on the night we first went out together; I felt rejected when you went out to the pub the night we got back from our honeymoon; I feel frustrated because you don't discuss financial decisions with me.)

_____

_____

_____

_____

_____

- When you have both finished, exchange your lists.

- Read silently the ways you have hurt each other.

- One of you then "reflect back" to your partner the reason for their hurt and the feelings it produced in them, without trying to interpret what they have written or to defend yourself. To clarify what they feel, ask questions such as: *"What did you mean by that?"* or *"Is there anything else you would like to say?"*

- Then the other partner should "reflect back" in the same way. Make sure each of you has an understanding of the feelings that are described.

- Return the lists to each other. Then add to or revise your list of the ways you have hurt your partner. Spend some time considering every aspect of their hurt. Try to see it through your partner's eyes.

- Throughout the coming week, allow God the opportunity to show you new insights into why your partner feels hurt and your part in causing it.

"Search me, O God, and know my heart; test me and know my anxious thoughts. See if there is any offensive way in me, and lead me in the way everlasting."
Psalm 139:23-24

- It is important to do the "Marriage Time Homework" in order to complete the process of *"getting rid of bitterness, rage and anger"* **(Ephesians 4:31)** by apologizing and forgiving.

Marriage Time Homework

If you have not done so, finish the exercise "Identifying unresolved hurt" on pages 51-53 and exchange lists as described on page 53.

Make sure you have at least two hours alone for Marriage Time this week.

EXERCISE – HEALING UNRESOLVED HURT

Do steps 1-4 on your own and then do steps 5-8 together.

1. Identify your partner's deepest hurt

Refer back to your list of your partner's hurts on page 52 and write down here the principal way in which you know you have hurt your husband/wife.

(For example: I hurt my husband/wife through making a joke about the misunderstanding between us; my husband/wife was hurt when I paid more attention to my work than to him/her.)

One of the principal ways I have hurt my husband/wife is:

_____

_____

_____

2. Try to understand your partner's feelings

With regard to this hurt, my husband/wife feels:

(For example: ridiculed, humiliated, unaffirmed, criticized, rejected, unloved, undervalued)

_____

_____

3. Recognize your responsibility (refuse to make excuses or to blame your husband or wife)

- I did it

- It was wrong

- I need to be forgiven by God and by my husband/wife

- I need to be prepared to change

"...now I am happy, not because you were made sorry, but because your sorrow led you to repentance. For you became sorrowful as God intended and so were not harmed in any way by us."
2 Corinthians 7:9

From now on, with God's help, I intend to:

_____

_____

_____

Now repeat steps 1-3 with any other ways you have hurt your husband/wife.

Please turn the page for steps 4 - 8.

(Turn page to continue)

4. Confess your sins to God

• Be specific

"Lord God, I have hurt you and my husband/wife by:

_____

_____

_____

_____

This was wrong and I ask You to forgive me. Thank You for taking my guilt on the cross and for giving me a new start. I ask You to help me to be the husband/ wife You want me to be."

• Believe God's promise of forgiveness and cleansing (see **1 John 1:9** on page 47)

5. Say sorry to each other

"I am so sorry for

_____

I know it hurts you and makes you feel

_____

From now on I intend to

_____

Please forgive me."

6. Forgive each other

- Say to your husband/wife, *"I forgive you"*

- For some people this is a struggle; it can be helpful first to express to God in writing our desire to forgive our husband/wife for particular hurts

e.g., Dear Lord, thank you that you know all about me and love me. Thank you for being ready to forgive me for the ways I have hurt others. You know how hurt and angry I felt when my husband/wife criticized me when I'd done my best. I choose to let go of my anger and resentment. I want to put my desire to retaliate into your hands, and ask you to help my husband/wife to change. I choose to forgive him/her as you have forgiven me. Please heal the hurt with your love.

"Forgive us our trespasses as we forgive those who trespass against us."
Luke 11:4

7. Comfort and pray for each other

- This is very valuable when you have made yourselves vulnerable to each other

- This brings healing to the hurt

"Confess your faults to one another and pray for one another so that you may be healed."
James 5:16

- Pray that your husband/wife will know freedom from guilt

8. Do something you both enjoy together

- In this way you will start to replace the negative emotions with positive ones

Notes

SESSION 5

Parents and In-laws

Reminder

The aim of *The Marriage Course* is to establish patterns of relating that will keep marriages alive for a lifetime.

Building strong foundations

- make marriage time a weekly priority in your planners

- meet each other's desires (see "Knowing me, knowing you" page 13)

The art of communication

- talk about your feelings with your partner this week

- listen to your partner's feelings without interrupting, criticizing, or offering advice

Resolving conflict

- express your appreciation for your partner every day

- when you disagree—discuss the issue rather than attack each other

- plan to spend a few minutes each day praying with and for each other

The power of forgiveness

- keep "the drain" clear of unresolved hurt and anger

- identify, apologize for, and forgive the ways you have hurt each other

PARENTS AND IN-LAWS

INTRODUCTION

- family background a big influence on marriage

- must leave behind parental control

- aim for a good relationship with parents and in-laws

- unresolved childhood pain must be addressed

- need to understand stages of family development

Notes

GROWING UP

1. Early years

Our parents' role:

- to meet our physical and emotional needs

- to set appropriate boundaries

- to show unconditional love

- to model a healthy relationship between themselves

2. Teenagers

Our parents' role:

- to give increasing independence

- to continue to meet our physical and emotional needs and set boundaries

- to show unconditional love

- to teach us to consider their needs and to start to give something back

3. Coming of age/leaving home

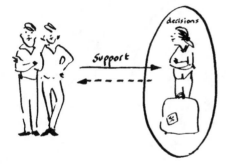

Our parents' role:

- to give support and advice (we may still have looked to our parental home for comfort, money, or help with the laundry!)

- to allow independence

- to make the transition to an adult relationship

4. Getting married

As a married couple, the independence must be complete.

We need to:

- establish our own home

- seek to meet each other's needs

- develop a relationship of mutual support with our parents and parents-in-law

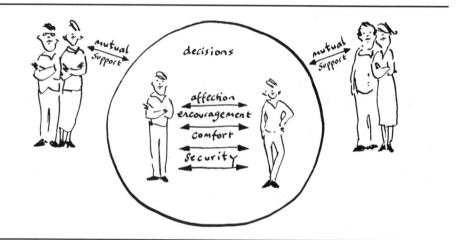

CREATING HEALTHY FAMILY RELATIONSHIPS

1. Resolve conflict

- all relationships involve some conflict

- the principles from Session 4—identify, apologize and forgive—apply to all close relationships

"For this reason a man will leave his mother and father...."
Genesis 2:24

- identify the issue causing tension and consider discussing it with parents/inlaws

- apologize for where you have gotten it wrong

- determine to forgive and move on

2. Consider their needs

- show gratitude to your parents

- don't abuse their availability

- maintain contact

  - take the initiative

  - telephone regularly

  - build a relationship for grandchildren

- give support

  - offer advice when needed

  - give practical help

  - consider living nearby/ together

3. Let go of emotional dependence on parents

- who is your "best friend"?

- timing and length of telephone calls

Notes

_____

_____

_____

_____

_____

_____

_____

_____

_____

_____

_____

_____

_____

_____

_____

_____

_____

_____

_____

"As far as it depends on you live at peace with everyone."
Romans 12:18

"Honor your father and your mother..."
Exodus 20:12

Notes

_____

_____

_____

_____

_____

_____

_____

_____

_____

_____

_____

_____

_____

_____

_____

_____

_____

_____

_____

4. Make your own decisions

- listen to their advice

- discuss issues with each other

5. Support each other

- resolve any confused loyalty

- agree on your policy and stand together

- resist interference

- help each other to draw boundaries if necessary

- never listen to criticism of your partner by your parents or in-laws

6. Have a realistic view of your parents

An adult relationship requires us to accept our parents as they are rather than as we would like them to be.

- be grateful for your parents' strengths

- recognize your parents' weaknesses

- consider the strengths and weaknesses of their relationship with each other

- be grateful for the needs your parents met for you

- recognize childhood needs that

were not met during your upbringing and any buried hurt and anger

Turn to pages 67-70 and complete the exercise "Reflect on your upbringing"

HEALING CHILDHOOD PAIN

1. Recognize unmet childhood needs and unresolved anger

Do not be surprised if you encounter strong feelings as you do this. Give God permission to open your heart and express your feelings to Him.

2. Grieve with each other

Allow your husband or wife to talk about what has been lost and give him/ her emotional support (*"...mourn with those who mourn."* **Romans 12:15**). Receive comfort from each other but do not demand it.

3. Forgive

Give up any desire to repay. Give up continuing expectations and longings of what you wanted your parents or others to be for you. Remember forgiveness is an ongoing act of the will.

Notes

_____

_____

_____

_____

_____

_____

_____

_____

_____

_____

_____

_____

_____

_____

_____

_____

_____

_____

_____

_____

_____

_____

_____

_____

Notes

_____

_____

_____

_____

_____

_____

_____

_____

_____

_____

_____

_____

_____

_____

_____

_____

_____

_____

_____

_____

_____

_____

4. Look to God and move on

Pray for yourself and each other. Ask God to heal the sense of loss and to help you to know His love. Dwell on the promises of God in the Bible, e.g., *"I have loved you with an everlasting love and am constant in My affection for you"* **Jeremiah 31: 3**. Believe God's unconditional love for you as you are now. Do not use childhood pain as an excuse for not meeting your partner's needs.

EXERCISE – Reflect on your upbringing

A. Your immediate family relationships

The big circle drawn below represents yourself. The coins on the table represent members of your immediate family.

1. Each of you spend three or four minutes arranging the coins according to the closeness of the relationships between your immediate family as you were growing up, where:

touching = *relationship (i.e., together with some communication)*

overlapping = *close relationship (i.e., good, open communication and conflict well resolved)*

separate = *lack of relationship (i.e., divorced, separated or no communication)*

2. Draw around the coins, marking in the names.

3. Look at each other's arrangements.

For example:

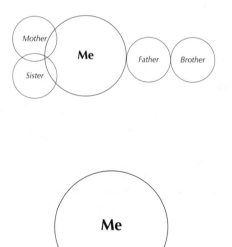

(Turn page to continue)

Please consider the following questions and check the relevant boxes:

B. Your parents'/step-parents' relationship with you

	Father or Step-father	Mother or Step-mother

Did your parents or step-parents:

• praise you as a child?	☐	☐
• meet your physical needs (for food, clothes, home, etc.)?	☐	☐
• give you a sense of security?	☐	☐
• respect your uniqueness?	☐	☐
• encourage you in your development?	☐	☐
• set clear rules/appropriate boundaries for you?	☐	☐
• give you increasing freedom appropriate to your age?	☐	☐
• comfort you when you were upset?	☐	☐
• give you presents?	☐	☐
• take an interest in your life?	☐	☐
• treat their children equally?	☐	☐
• admit their mistakes and apologize when necessary?	☐	☐
• forgive you for your mistakes?	☐	☐
• have realistic expectations of what was appropriate for your age?	☐	☐

	Father or Step-father	Mother or Step-mother
• accept your friends?	☐	☐
• help you relate well to your siblings and peers?	☐	☐
• establish clear family rules?	☐	☐
• give discipline in a consistent, fair way?	☐	☐
• spend ample time with you (i.e., play with you, talk to you, etc.)?	☐	☐
• show you physical affection (i.e., hug you, kiss you, etc.)?	☐	☐

C. Your parents'/step-parents' relationship with each other

	Yes	Sometimes	No	Don't know
Did your parents or step-parents:				
• have a strong loving relationship?	☐	☐	☐	☐
• show interest in each other?	☐	☐	☐	☐
• have fun together regularly?	☐	☐	☐	☐
• spend time together on their own?	☐	☐	☐	☐
• show each other physical affection?	☐	☐	☐	☐
• help each other in small and big tasks?	☐	☐	☐	☐
• encourage each other with praise and appreciation?	☐	☐	☐	☐
• show each other respect?	☐	☐	☐	☐

(Turn page to continue)

	Yes	Sometimes	No	Don't know
• communicate honestly and directly?	☐	☐	☐	☐
• listen to each other without interrupting or criticizing?	☐	☐	☐	☐
• resolve conflicts effectively?	☐	☐	☐	☐
• apologize to and forgive each other when appropriate?	☐	☐	☐	☐
• agree on the use of their money?	☐	☐	☐	☐
• give each other presents?	☐	☐	☐	☐
• have mutual interests?	☐	☐	☐	☐
• show a willingness to negotiate?	☐	☐	☐	☐
• remain faithful to each other?	☐	☐	☐	☐

When you have finished A, B, and C above, please discuss the following questions together:

- What do you need to be grateful for from your upbringing?

- Did you have any unmet childhood needs?

- Are you aware of these adversely affecting your marriage?

- Are you aware of benefits to your marriage/family life through imitating your parents?

- Are you aware of ways you adversely affect your marriage/family life through imitating your parents?

Marriage Time Homework

EXERCISE – Relating to Parents

A. Being aware of the past

Spend ten minutes filling in your "Life Graph" overleaf as in the example below.

- Record the most significant events that come to mind.

- Put positive experiences, graded between 0 and +100, above the "neutral line."

- Put negative experiences, graded between 0 and –100, below the "neutral line."

- Show your husband or wife what you have put.

- Consider whether you have been able to forgive those who have hurt you.

- Tell your husband or wife what you felt then and what you feel now about these events.

- Where one of you has been hurt by others during your upbringing, check that you are both going through the four steps for "Healing childhood pain" (pages 65 and 66).

Example:

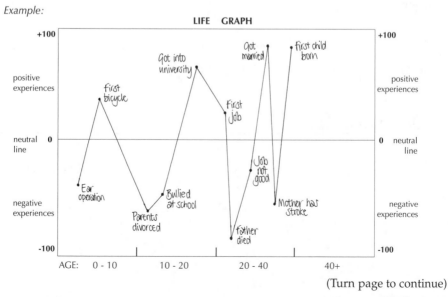

LIFE   GRAPH

(Turn page to continue)

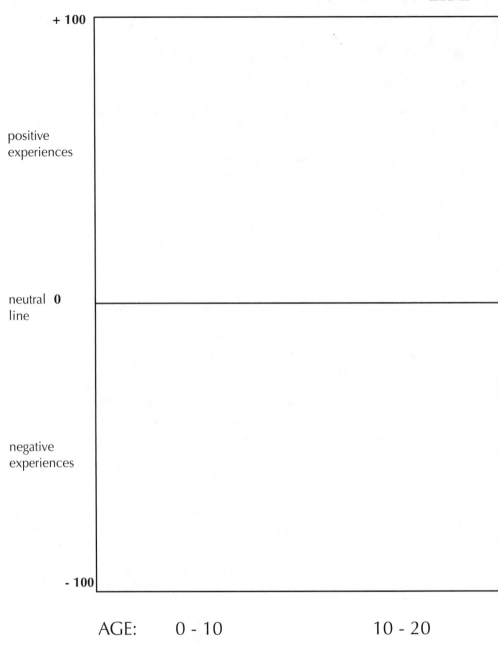

+ 100

positive
experiences

neutral **0**
line

negative
experiences

- 100

AGE: 0 - 10   10 - 20

GRAPH

+ 100

positive
experiences

0 neutral
line

negative
experiences

- 100

20 - 40   40+

(Turn page to continue)

B. Supporting each other

Each of you should fill in the following questions on your own, and then exchange your answers. Please consider carefully what your partner has written. Discuss the significant issues—pay particular attention to an issue that your partner has highlighted and you have not. You may need to adjust some of your own answers as a result.

1. Do your parents (seek to) control or interfere in your decisions and the direction of your lives? If so, specify in what ways.

_____

_____

_____

2. Is there an unhealthy emotional dependence between you and a parent, or your partner and a parent? If so, in what way?

_____

_____

_____

3. Are there issues relating to your parents (in-laws) that cause tension or arguments between you?

For example: "There is often tension between us when I have spent a long time on the telephone with one of my parents."

_____

_____

_____

4. In what way could you support your partner with regard to your parents and in-laws?

_____

_____

_____

5. In what way could your partner support you with regard to your parents and in-laws?

_____

_____

_____

6. Do you or your partner have unmet childhood needs? If so, how could you help your partner?

_____

_____

_____

How could your partner help you?

_____

_____

_____

(Turn page to continue)

C. Supporting your parents

1. How could you express your gratitude toward your parents (and/or parents-in-law)?

_____

_____

_____

2. How can you best keep in touch with your parents (and/or parents-in-law)?

Consider telephone calls, timing and length of visits, and other ways of communicating with them.

_____

_____

_____

3. Consider the needs of your parents and parents in-law.

From the list opposite, check the relevant boxes for the needs of both your parents and parents-in-law. Then write beside the boxes you have checked the ways you could help meet those needs.

Husband's parent(s)   **Wife's parent(s)**

NEEDS:

Husband's parent(s)		Wife's parent(s)
☐	Advice	☐
☐	Companionship	☐
☐	Conversation	☐
☐	Encouragement	☐
☐	Practical help	☐
☐	Security	☐
☐	Understanding	☐
☐	other need	☐
☐	other need	☐

SESSION 6

Good Sex

Reminder

The aim of *The Marriage Course* is to establish patterns of relating that will keep marriages alive for a lifetime.

Building strong foundations

- make marriage time a weekly priority in your planners

- meet each other's desires (see "Knowing me, knowing you," page 13)

The art of communication

- talk about your feelings with your partner this week

- listen to your partner's feelings without interrupting, criticizing, or offering advice

Resolving conflict

- express your appreciation for your partner every day

- when you disagree, discuss the issue rather than attack each other

- plan to spend a few minutes each day praying with and for each other

The power of forgiveness

- keep "the drain" clear of unresolved hurt and anger

- identify, apologize for, and forgive the ways you have hurt each other

Parents and in-laws

- be sure you have left your parents—together make your own decisions and support each other

- let go of unresolved anger from your upbringing through forgiveness and prayer

GOOD SEX

INTRODUCTION

How we view sex makes all the difference

1. Our consumer society

- sex largely divorced from relationship and intimacy

- seeking instant gratification

- assumption that enjoyment wanes with familiarity

Notes

_____

_____

_____

_____

_____

_____

_____

_____

_____

_____

_____

_____

_____

_____

_____

_____

_____

_____

_____

_____

_____

_____

Notes

_____

_____

_____

_____

_____

_____

_____

_____

_____

_____

_____

_____

_____

_____

_____

_____

_____

_____

_____

_____

_____

_____

_____

_____

_____

_____

_____

_____

_____

_____

_____

_____

_____

_____

_____

_____

_____

_____

_____

_____

_____

_____

_____

_____

_____

_____

"I am my lover's and my lover is mine..." **Song of Songs 6:3**

- often tarnished by guilt

2. God's truth on sex is wonderful

- a gift from God for our pleasure and enjoyment within a marriage relationship (see **Song of Songs**)

- a way of communicating love that goes beyond words

- to express and deepen the "one flesh" relationship

- to grow over a lifetime of developing intimacy

3. A vital part of a marriage relationship

- not the icing on the cake but a vital ingredient

- not to be compartmentalized

- sexual intimacy affects every other part of our marriage and vice versa

- often the first casualty to tiredness or laziness

- may need to make lifestyle changes, e.g., exercise, change eating habits

4. Problems can be worked through

- most problems resolved through a better understanding and making changes

- some involve deeper issues from the past—God is able to heal and restore, through prayer and a specialist's help

SIX QUALITIES FOR GREAT LOVERS

1. The importance of communication

- difficult at first because deeply private and requires vulnerability

- differences between male and female sexuality

- each person unique and will change over a marriage

- tell each other what you enjoy—don't leave to guess work

- bring fears out into the open

2. The importance of tenderness

- take time over lovemaking

- tune in to each other's emotional needs

- resolve conflict first

- increase nonsexual touching—holding hands, arm around a shoulder, etc.

Notes

_____

_____

_____

_____

_____

_____

_____

_____

_____

_____

_____

_____

_____

_____

_____

_____

_____

_____

_____

_____

"His left arm is under my head, and his right arm embraces me."
Song of Songs 2:6

Notes

_____

_____

_____

_____

_____

_____

_____

_____

_____

_____

_____

Lover: "You are a garden locked up... my bride you are a spring enclosed, a sealed fountain."
Beloved: "Awake, north wind, and come, south wind! Blow on my garden, that its fragrance may spread abroad. Let my lover come into his garden and taste its choice fruits." **Song of Songs 4:12 & 16**

"Finally, brothers and sisters, whatever is true, whatever is noble, whatever is right, whatever is pure, whatever is lovely, whatever is admirable—if anything is excellent or praiseworthy—think about such things." **Philippians 4:8**

3. The importance of responsiveness

- discover how to "unlock the garden" (**Song of Songs 4:12**)

- accept your own and each other's body—do not compare to current fashion

- a lifetime of exploration and discovery

- growing together not judging each other

4. The importance of romance

- creates the setting for lovemaking

- the antidote to mechanical sex

- learn the art of seduction and arousal

- take the initiative

5. The importance of anticipation

- our mind is the most important sexual resource

- the best sex starts at breakfast

- direct thoughts toward your partner

- the danger of pornography

- the danger of fantasizing

6. The importance of variety

- familiarity breeds complacency

- creativity produces excitement

- try a different place

- vary the time

- experiment with atmosphere—sexuality and sensuality

- vary the routine—read a book together

Turn to pages 85-89 and complete the exercise—"Talking about sex"

PROTECTING OUR MARRIAGE

- the allure of the affair

- the effects on family life

1. Build each other up

- danger of failing to meet each other's emotional needs

2. Set boundaries

- control thoughts

3. Talk to someone about the feelings

- the effects of secrecy

"... at our door is every delicacy, both new and old, that I have stored up for you, my lover."
Song of Songs 7:13

"I tell you that anyone who looks at a woman lustfully has already committed adultery with her in his heart."
Matthew 5:28

Notes

_____

_____

_____

_____

_____

_____

_____

_____

_____

_____

_____

4. Keep sex alive

- the effect of tiredness
- address problems
- the effects of having children

"Place me like a seal over your heart, like a seal on your arm; for love is a strong as death, its jealousy unyielding as the grave. It burns like blazing fire, like a mighty flame. Many waters cannot quench love; rivers cannot wash it away. If one were to give all the wealth of one's house for love it would be utterly scorned."
Song of Songs 8:6-7

"So guard yourself in your spirit and do not break faith."
Malachi 2:16

EXERCISE – Talking about sex

Please fill in sections A, B, and C individually.

A. Rate your lovemaking

Against the list of six qualities below, circle the number against each category—for yourself (A) and for your husband or wife (B)—which you feel best describes your sexual relationship, where 1 = not so good and 5 = very good:

A You					Qualities	B Your partner				
1	2	3	4	5	Communication	1	2	3	4	5
1	2	3	4	5	Tenderness	1	2	3	4	5
1	2	3	4	5	Responsiveness	1	2	3	4	5
1	2	3	4	5	Romance	1	2	3	4	5
1	2	3	4	5	Anticipation	1	2	3	4	5
1	2	3	4	5	Variety	1	2	3	4	5

Which area(s) do you need to work on?

_____

_____

B. Identify problem areas

1. What, if any, are the differences between you, as husband and wife, in the way you respond sexually?

_____

_____

(Turn page to continue)

Are these differences having a positive or negative effect on your marriage?

_____

If positive, give the main reason:

_____

If negative, give the main reason:

_____

2. Does your self-esteem and body image affect your lovemaking negatively?

_____

If so, explain why:

_____

_____

How could your husband or wife help you?

_____

_____

3. What, if any, unresolved emotions (such as resentment, hurt, unforgiveness, anxiety, or guilt) affect your lovemaking in any way?

_____

_____

If so, how?

_____

_____

How could these be resolved?

_____

_____

4. Does your lovemaking lack excitement?

_____

If so, what new element would you like to see introduced?

_____

_____

5. Does over-tiredness take a toll on the frequency of your lovemaking?

_____

If so, identify the reason for over-tiredness:

_____

_____

(Turn page to continue)

What could re-energize you? *(e.g, exercise, better communication, resolving past hurt, planning and prioritizing sex, more sleep, less going out, more fun and less work)*

_____

_____

6. Do you feel free to talk together about your lovemaking?

_____

If the answer is yes, write down two or three things your husband or wife has told you recently that have enhanced your lovemaking:

_____

_____

If the answer is no, identify some of the reasons for your difficulty:

_____

_____

Suggest something you would like your husband or wife to say that you have never heard:

_____

_____

C. Write the script

List below the different criteria that would create for you a good time of lovemaking.

Be specific about such things as timing, taking the initiative, anticipation, position, atmosphere, place, romance, tenderness, seduction, and arousal (foreplay), afterward. (We cannot guess each other's expectations.)

1.	7.
2.	8.
3.	9.
4.	10.
5.	11.
6.	12.

D. Seek to understand each other better

- Once you have finished, read each other's responses to sections A, B, and C.

- Now start to talk about what the other has expressed—beginning where you feel most comfortable.

- Give each other the opportunity to ask questions about what you have written. Tell your husband or wife what surprised you most. Ask for clarification if you do not fully understand.

(Turn page to continue)

Marriage Time Homework

Happiness and fulfillment in this area of our marriage will depend on meeting our husband or wife's needs, as we would like them to meet ours. Be careful not to push your partner to fulfill your desires—look to meet theirs.

- Plan times of making love (even if it seems contrived at first) to fulfill what you both feel comfortable with from Section C of the exercise "Talking about sex" (page 89).

SESSION 7

Love in Action

(The following notes are based on *The Five Love Languages* by Gary Chapman, published by Northfield, 1992)

THE FIVE EXPRESSIONS OF LOVE

INTRODUCTION

There are five ways through which we can express love:

1. Loving words

2. Thoughtful presents

3. Physical affection

4. Quality time

5. Kind actions

- these expressions are like languages that communicate love

- for each of us one of these "love languages" will communicate love more effectively than the others

- often different for our partner

- common to try to communicate love in the way we understand it and want to receive it

Notes

_____

_____

_____

_____

_____

_____

_____

_____

_____

_____

_____

_____

_____

_____

_____

_____

_____

_____

_____

_____

"Pleasant words are a honeycomb, sweet to the soul and healing to the bones."
Proverbs 16:24

- learn which expressions of love are most important to your partner

- practice using them

LOVING WORDS

Words have great power either to build up or to undermine our partner.

- words of appreciation

  (see Session 4, page 36)

- words of encouragement

- words of kindness

- making requests not demands

For some, hearing words of affirmation feels like arriving at an oasis in a desert.

THOUGHTFUL PRESENTS

Presents are visual symbols of love. This expression of love is the easiest to learn but we may need to change our attitude to money. Giving presents is a way of investing in our marriage.

- can be inexpensive but have high value

- don't wait for special occasions

- discover what your partner likes (within your budget!)

PHYSICAL AFFECTION

Touch is a powerful communicator of love in marriage.

- can speak louder than words

- takes many different forms—holding hands, an arm round a shoulder or waist, a kiss, a hug, a hand on a hand, a brush of the body as you pass, a back massage, sexual foreplay, making love

- sexual and nonsexual touch are important

- men and women function differently

- for many wives, touch and signs of affection have little to do with sex

- for some husbands, touch is simply part of sexual arousal

- learn ways to give nonsexual touch

If this is your partner's primary way of feeling loved, in times of crisis touch will communicate more than anything else that you care.

Notes

"To touch my body is to touch me. To withdraw from my body is to distance yourself from me emotionally."
Gary Chapman

Notes

_____

_____

_____

_____

_____

_____

_____

_____

_____

_____

_____

_____

_____

_____

_____

_____

_____

_____

_____

_____

"Do to others as you would have them do to you."
Luke 6:31

QUALITY TIME

Married couples can spend much time together without using it to convey love to their partners. Togetherness does not just require physical proximity. It involves our focused attention. The following are only developed with quality time spent together:

- communication (literally = making thoughts common between people)

    – some must learn to listen
    – others must learn to talk

- companionship (literally = taking bread together)

    – mealtimes are especially important

- comradeship (literally = being together in the same place)

    – friendship is built around shared activities and shared memories

KIND ACTIONS

This involves expressing love through serving someone, through seeking to meet their needs in practical ways.

- routine acts of service—meeting regular needs

- nonroutine—responding to a particular need at a particular time

- may be requested but should not be demanded nor taken for granted

- must be careful not to limit serving and helping each other to stereotypes copied from our parents or from the prevailing culture

CONCLUSION

Jesus Christ showed love in all five ways:

- words

"As the Father has loved Me, so have I loved you."
John 15: 9

- time

"Come with Me by yourselves to a quiet place."
Mark 6: 31

- actions

"He poured some water into a basin and began to wash His disciples' feet."
John 13:5

- touch

"Jesus reached out His hand and touched the man."
Luke 5: 13

Notes

_____

_____

_____

_____

_____

_____

_____

_____

_____

_____

_____

_____

_____

_____

_____

_____

_____

_____

_____

*"My command is this: Love each
other as I have loved you."*
John 15:12

• presents

*"Jesus took the loaves, gave thanks,
and distributed to those who were
seated as much as they wanted."*
John 6:11

Love is not just a feeling—it
requires an act of the will to meet
each other's needs. We are called
to imitate and obey Jesus.

EXERCISE – Discover your partner's and your own "love language(s)"

Please do questions 1 and 2 on your own and then share your responses.

1. Write down, for each other, up to 12 specific occasions through which you have known your partner's love for you. (It could be at any stage in your relationship—before or after marriage. These may be regular or rare events and could be deemed of major or minor significance.)

I have known your love for me when:

For example:

- *We sat under the stars talking about our future when we were going out.*
- *You gave me that watch on our wedding anniversary.*
- *You cooked a special meal for my birthday*
- *You said how proud you were of me when I was promoted.*
- *You spontaneously put your arm around me when we were waiting for the film to start.*

- _____
- _____
- _____
- _____
- _____
- _____
- _____
- _____
- _____
- _____
- _____
- _____

(Turn page to continue)

2. Taking into consideration your answers to question 1, put the five ways of showing love in order of importance for you, where 1 = most important and 5 = least important. Then consider in which order of importance you think they come for your partner.

For you (number 1 – 5)	Love Languages	For your partner (number 1-5)
	Loving words	
	Thoughtful presents	
	Physical affection	
	Quality time	
	Kind actions	

3. Now, compare and discuss with your husband or wife what each of you put for questions 1 and 2.

4. Looking at your partner's first "love language" (i.e., the most important), list three ways in which you could communicate love to your husband or wife this week or this month.

(Try to keep within the bounds of reality!)

(1) _____

(2) _____

(3) _____

5. Looking at your partner's second "love language" (i.e., the second most important), list three more ways in which you could communicate love to your husband or wife effectively this week or this month.

(1) _____

(2) _____

(3) _____

6. Experiment and see what the results are!

Marriage Time Homework

EXERCISE – Putting it into practice

1. Five things I especially want to remember and practice from *The Marriage Course*:

1. _____

2. _____

3. _____

4. _____

5. _____

Show your husband or wife what you have written.

2. Now ask him/her, "What five things would you especially like me to remember and practice from *The Marriage Course*?" Write them down here:

1. _____

2. _____

3. _____

4. _____

5. _____

The Marriage Course checklist

Go through the following list on a regular basis, perhaps once a month, to be reminded of issues raised on *The Marriage Course*. Whenever you cannot answer "yes" to one of the questions below, refer back to the relevant session of *The Marriage Course*.

	Answer "yes"/"no" or "uncertain"	If "no" or "uncertain" refer back to Session:
1. Are you booking in "marriage time" each week?		1
2. Have you met your husband or wife's top three desires this week?		1
3. Have you talked about your feelings with your husband or wife this week?		2
4. Have you listened to your husband's or wife's feelings this week without interrupting, criticizing, or offering advice?		2
5. Have you expressed your appreciation for your husband or wife today?		3
6. At times of conflict, are you discussing the issue rather than attacking each other?		3
7. Have you taken time to listen to your husband's or wife's point of view (especially if you are a natural "rhino")?		3

(Turn page to continue)

	Answer "yes"/"no" or "uncertain"	If "no" or "uncertain" refer back to Session:
8. Have you spent a few minutes today praying with and for each other, or expressed your support in another way?		3
9. Have you talked about your hurts with your husband or wife (especially if you are a natural "hedgehog")?		4
10. Have you apologized to your husband or wife recently?		4
11. Have you forgiven your husband or wife for any ways he/she has hurt you?		4
12. Are you maintaining independence of your parents and parents-in-law?		5
13. Have you forgiven your parents or any others for ways they have hurt you or failed you?		5
14. Have you made love this week in a way that communicated your love and commitment to each other?		6
15. Have you shown love to your husband or wife this week according to their first "love language"?		7

	Answer "yes"/"no" or "uncertain"	If "no" or uncertain" refer back to Session:
16. Have you shown love to your husband or wife this week according to their second "love language"?		7

If you are interested in more information about *The Marriage Course* please contact one of the following:

Alpha U.S.A.
74 Trinity Place
New York, NY 10006
Tel: 800 DO ALPHA
Tel: 800.362.5742
Fax: 212.406.7521
e-mail: marriagecourse@alphausa.org
www.marriagecourseusa.org

Alpha Canada
Suite #230 – 11331 Coppersmith Way
Riverside Business Park
Richmond, BC V7A 5J9
Tel: 800.743.0899
Fax: 604.271.6124
e-mail: registrar@themarriagecourse.ca
www.www.themarriagecourse.ca

To purchase resources in Canada:

Cook Communications Ministries
P.O. Box 98, 55 Woodslee Avenue
Paris, ONT N3L 3E5
Tel: 800.263.2664
Fax: 800.461.8575
e-mail: custserv@cook.ca
www.cook.ca